Burning like Her Own Planet

Burning like Her Own Planet

VANDANA KHANNA

Alice James Books
New Gloucester, Maine
alicejamesbooks.org
CELEBRATING 50 YEARS OF ALICE JAMES BOOKS

10 9 8 7 6 5 4 3 2 1

Alice James Books are published by Alice James Poetry Cooperative, Inc.

Alice James Books
Auburn Hall
60 Pineland Drive, Suite 206
New Gloucester, ME 04260
www.alicejamesbooks.org

Library of Congress Cataloging-in-Publication Data

Names: Khanna, Vandana, 1972- author.
Title: Burning like her own planet / Vandana Khanna.
Description: New Gloucester, ME : Alice James Books, [2023]
Identifiers: LCCN 2022041562 (print) | LCCN 2022041563 (ebook) | ISBN
    9781949944518 (trade paperback) | ISBN 9781949944242 (epub)
Subjects: LCSH: Hindu goddesses--Poetry. | LCGFT: Poetry.
Classification: LCC PS3611.H36 B87 2023 (print) | LCC PS3611.H36 (ebook)
    | DDC 811/.6--dc23/eng/20220919
LC record available at https://lccn.loc.gov/2022041562
LC ebook record available at https://lccn.loc.gov/2022041563

Alice James Books gratefully acknowledges support from individual donors, private foun-
dations, the National Endowment for the Arts, and the Amazon Literary Partnership.

Cover Image by Hanifa F. Abdul Hameed

Contents

Tell it slant

—Emily Dickinson

Thou bringest me—
a mingled draught of bliss and pain

—The Rāmāyana, Valmiki

Goddess Erasure

He approached   alone   in the forest
the   darkness   cruel

came closer   like a planet   towards

a constellation in   absence of the moon

Even the trees   dared not move

Prayer to Recognize the Body

There must be a word for this
heart-growing, to explain

these teeth, stinging like a gift—
tremble of sweat coaxed from scalp

and flesh. The next thing I covet:
the third eye's velvet blink, the green

pulse in my veins of a forest
I can't make myself step

out of. And what of all the things
remade, swabbed free of salt?

Because who can tell the difference
in the dark between antlers and branches

and bone, between the thick-haired
chest of an animal and you?

Part I

Hindu Mythology in Shorthand

Begin with the blue god with
the charm, the flute, and the cows.

Then the holy monkey who
thrashes through the jungle

crushing everything lush and green
underfoot. I'm seven and can't sleep

because it's not Virginia, it's not
snowing. The stories in Sanskrit,

in Hindi—jumbled and cloudy
in my ears. My grandmother

wants me to forget it's Christmas
in India, tells of Durga riding

a tiger, arms filled with sickles
and swords: vindication manifest

in the steel's sharp edges. Of stolen
Sita selfless and pure, the sag of her

mud-streaked sari I imagined
the color of unused sky, green

of Himalayan summers, but it was
probably red, like every other one

I'd seen since I'd gotten off
the airplane—shades of crimson,

shades of bleeding. There was
that smell—Delhi?—that I couldn't

sniff out of my nose: incense and
sandalwood, husked corn and lemons,

the tar of oily streets and burning
tires following me through

roadside stalls and halal markets
down rows of henna and biscuits

caught in the crease of my neck
in the bucket of bath water, on

the cotton pillow sown with tiny
mirrors reflecting back bits of myself.

Then the holy charioteers pinned
the sky with arrows of fire and we

sang *OM* and *Ram, Ram,* me trying
to make it sound like it was born in

my mouth, my third eye awake behind
the skull's delicate cradle, blinking.

Fable

You want a girl who'll let you cry in her
hair, who isn't afraid of the forest at dark—
its black-eyed beasts, backbiting teeth.

My hand in yours is for pretend, for fable.
With you, I'm as close to woman as I'll
ever be, practicing my pout, posing prim.

I can prance like a golden deer
when the music starts. I'll have you
begging at my hem, forgetting all

your prayers. I'll let the birds build
nests out of your lies. The only words
left on your tongue will be *salt*

and *sorrow*, the only stars you won't
know how to read will be mine.

Creation Myth

This is how the whole holy mess
went down: cue the girl in tone-deaf
gold, drama thick in her blood, a kind
of love always caught in the underworld
or the other world, all vendetta and Vedas.
She woke from dreams silted with arrows,
broken teeth, the man-smell still sharp
and human on her, the birds nearsighted
with melancholy, her heart wintering
over some god she'll probably never
see again. He tells her to play dead, that
no one will notice—just another girl
from some hill town with her lotus-petal
eyes walking into a forest on fire.

Why Sita Is Chosen

Amongst peacocks and jacaranda
she is common, calls everything

leaf, bird, sky. The forest left its
branches in her chest, mobbed

her dreams with its noise, its
fisted heat. She wakes in

the wrong season to a mouth full
of pine needles, winter grass,

imagines the cold hush of stars
luminescent as spiked halos, as

proof. Wary of fire, she backs away
from stove, candle, match. In mirrors,

she sees only a yielding—practices
bending to the wind.

Monologue for a Goddess in Her First Incarnation

Invent me in the half-opened eye
of night, stripped down to the brown
of my mind, the wind at my back,

a dark claw. Tell me again
I am unforgettable: face losing
composition—the blue tint

of a stranger, spine whittled
to shadow, to hum, until I am
a see-through goddess. Undone,

my body can't remember itself:
somber knots and stem, bright stalks
of bone. Husband, for you, I go to pieces.

On the Eve of Being Reincarnated

Held together by sap and spiderweb,
nettles caught on hem and hair—
I'm one good incarnation away

from disaster. Poised for tragedy
against the deadlocked trees, I
don't disappoint. On this night

of about-to-be, let me be mended—
shine like a new scar, become one
goddess, and then another, one wife,

then: take my hand, find our story
where the lines meet.

Sita's First Kiss with Suburban Landscape

In our seventh incarnation, we find
each other tethered by fence and sidewalk
shoulders in sunlight, husked throats
swollen with new breath.

Our mouths meet in small disasters.
You taste of all the people you've already
been: salted stubble, forehead a field shorn clean.

Blank-palmed and desperate, we wait
for a lotus to bloom from your navel,
our faces pollen-dusted against suburban sky.

Abandoned to an unruly yard, we are
destined to repeat—lips then sky, then
fume of mosquitoes in the prickled heat
of the porch until we become restless
in a haze of honeysuckle and wasp.

For Some Girls It's Impossible

It takes a lifetime to walk into
that jungle and let the animals smell
the rain-throb of your skin, songs
of burning line your throat black,
make you forget the music
your own voice makes.

You can't ignore the ache deep
in the wooded muscle of your heart—
a territory you divide and light
to keep the dark away, to thaw
the sweetness from your blood.

Take his name in vain because
it's the only one you know, because
it's his heart you will waste time
mending. Your bones ready
to dissemble, mind already aflame.

Someone, hand this girl a match.

In Captivity, Sita Contemplates Fidelity

I search the bleak sky for shine.
My thoughts a thin prickle
pecked by days of jungle rain—
the sound of waiting a white blur.

What is the color of devotion?
Purple night. Greened jungles,
yellow marigold dust.

And still, I will not let anyone
touch me, my knotted braid imagines
itself a slick river in your hands,
the pleats of my sari—crisp, patient.

I refused that monkey you sent.
My rescue is only yours: through
meadow and leaf, wide-armed branches
snatching at your back.

Once, you pulled the sky so close
we could feel its humid silk after monsoon—
our fingers wet with melancholy.

Husband, every night is yours:
fill it with the bow's tight snap,
the hollow whistle of arrows on fire.

When I close my eyes, I can hear
the dusk burning from the sky.

Sita in Exile

Before the forest, giving in was easy:
my hands for your prayers, my skin
for your mouth. But once your doubt
grew taut, it was all fire: my ruin begun

in dirt and rubble, fourteen years
of leering branches, of stars plotting
against me. Now, I sleep alone
in the sweat of the afternoon, waken

to an evening peeled open. I bless all
that is seen and unseen with a bucket
of river water: under the rough of my hair,
in the quiet between arms and thighs.

Gaunt as paper, I wander the walled
garden, pull my melancholy close,
a numb shawl. I beckon the tiger
to come and lick my ankles free of ash.

Goddess in the Dark

You kept me hidden in a drawer
of wilt and weeds, seeds sprouting sour:
where you left the tiger, the ash, our story.

Fire always the prerequisite to love.

What a way to treat a lady. I stayed midnight
to midnight, the air a stubborn gem of black,

bowed my head and practiced how to hold
the moon's broken bowl in my hands.

The silver sprigs of light slipping through
my woven fingers I mistake for holiness.

I never catch enough to make it day.

The thorn's deft stabs in the dark mark
our love in hot scratches, leave my

happiness scabbed, tough to the touch.
I choke down my prayers, the only
way I know how to be.

A world like this hates

a girl on her own, spiderwebbed, bones
all out of place, a rented soul
on the fritz. There was one browner
than me, pushed into the corner, ginger
and bitter roots growing at her ankles.

You whitewashed, all halos and bees
and time, me with my pried-open prayers
full of silt—all I wanted: a bit of ruby
on my lips, someone to smooth the sharp
thorn of my head, a body that hums
in contrary light.

I can pull the stars, their bright aching,
from the sky—but I can't dream all
the leaves back onto the trees.

Goddess Banished

Don't think I didn't hear you
throw my name around to your boys.

How you tried to muddy it in the river
when I wasn't looking.

My mother warned me not to walk
into that jungle with you, but I liked
the way you held the world together
with your teeth.

Some things a girl can't get over—
how you left me without a place to sit
with wet-slop winter in my blood,
the universe gone and changed
with the soft heat of your dreams.

By day, you were all sweet in the mouth,
saying you could turn anyone holy.
By night, the bride's red faded
from my hands like an old bleed.

That ugly river's tongue—
its chore, all along, was to divide us.

Sita Considers Her Rebellions

She remembers from inside the story,
inside the forest's heat (a flush of green):
a dowry of twigs, tree trunks thick as lies.

When she is allowed, she misses herself,
covets the clean corners where her bones
meet, the soft pulse of her tongue on his.

All those misplaced stars, a misery
she can't find. She has killed things
(though it is forbidden) with her hands

(the wedding mehndi long-faded),
has eaten on the wrong day, forgotten
to fast. She has pulled the strings

of the jungle behind her like a black net,
a wide-mouthed yawn. She holds it tight
so it can't grow when she isn't looking.

Destruction Myth

A ransom of tangled sari, broken gold,
this girl holds the hush of loam and leaf,
the soil's damp-breathed kiss. Once,

I was untouched and still you asked
for proof: my feet on fire-threaded coals,
soft as lotus petals. Pressed into the ground

I dissolve into silt, into cloth, the lucky
one: blessed by gravel and dust, a pretty
neck strung with pebbles.

My virtue becomes a heavy hem pulled
down, dirty blooms choked into the slender
vase of my throat. Bury me with my hurt:

skinned and spare, with my voice sooty
with black strands, flecked bone.

Name Calling

Of all the things you named,
I wasn't one of them. Plain-

faced in a field full of pretty, I
wasted years wandering a world

that forgot to give me the time
of day. All that dirt and animal

just to reach you. Call me a faker,
goddess-impersonator, dripping

in old gold and sweat. Even when
I repeat all the words to your prayers

with my red-bride mouth, you tell
me to get lost—for real, forever,

insist on sending in a god to light
me quick as a fickle flame.

Self-Portrait as Goddess after the Fire

My heart is no lantern.
No matter what they tell you,
it's not all marigolds and *Ram, Ram*
like some Hindu cheerleading chant.

At first, all I wanted was fire:
soot-lined face, hair in needles
of light and heat, the tight fist
of lungs like a blazing hive.

Red flame, blue flame—it was all the same.

But then, right before my bones
flared like torchlight, blistered fingertips
smoothed to a shine, I thought
of the cool cusp of the moon,

river water soothing my throat,
a muddy womb contracting
around me—muck and silt
lining my mouth like a new word

for smoke, for freedom.

Instead, I have cinder cupped
into the curve of my body, all
this worthless ash.

Part II

Goddess Erasure

O goddess,
        you are the altar   the sacrifice

May she,   rich in milk,   be drained for us

Creation Myth

You're a different kind of girl, one
only a god could love, one the animals
spurn because they like you better lonely.

Creation isn't for the faint of heart.

Let him fashion you from sandalwood,
stardust, and soap, from navel and seed.

Give up all the thin hymns you once knew.
Become a bird that never shuts up, a river
that won't flood with drama.

Become a tangle of wives, the tight clutch
of girls, a swarm of goddesses.

Wake from the tiger in your dreams
and with all the hands you are given,
pull at the thick, gold scruff of this world.

Parvati Practices Her Austerities

The first thing to go: the word *soft*,
the clean teeth of a comb, the color red.

Then, I forget what I look like, or don't
care: weave twigs in my hair for clips,

make believe mushrooms are pearls, sheathe
my feet in slippers of dried mud. I teach

myself to hold the hum of *OM* in my lungs
until I'm holy, until you open your eyes

and see I am an empty bowl careful
with my wanting. I can wind the hot

gnaw of hunger into a tight spool, body
ready to snap, ready to sing any song

you want from the thin reed of my throat.
My narrowing proves all I've given up.

Look for me: a bone-white sari wrung free
of this world. Tell me this time I'll get what I want.

The Mother-Goddess Advises

Watch out for the one with the pink cheeks,
with wrists that can twist to music.
She wants you for the wrong reason:
the way the blue of your skin reminds
her of the sky after a monsoon.

Resist her tender shoulder, the smooth
slope of back. Resist her slim ankles
her milk-scent, her wonder.

You can name every flower, every
animal in the darkening forest, and she—
simple, only calls out the obvious:
marigold, peacock, bull.

The Mother-Goddess Speaks
of Her Regrets

Stiff with losing—child after child unfurls
from me—each one a peacock feather, each

one turned to air before I can name it. All
except for you—my last one, my blue one.

At first push, lightning puckered the night
sky my body leaked over the prison floor

like the moon's cold drizzle to dawn,
my womb swept clean for the last time.

I can already smell the cow's milk
on your skin, the wet grass and marigolds

where you will roam. When you arrive,
animals shine yellow with turmeric:

your birth announced not as a god, but a boy,
son of a herder. Your whole life in disguise.

Now every time the wind rustles, I know it's
your flute calling over hillsides and rivers

across fields of rice—a world away. My ears
how they prick, how they lie.

Novice

No one wished me well: too plain
or too pretty, sadness buzzed around
me like a hot swathe of wasps.

I was the wrong wife, the wrong
goddess, last in line, a trophy pinned
with dead flowers and scorn—examined

by moonlight, flashlight, the gaps between
my bones gathering to a weak glimmer.
Try, but no chant will keep me

in my place; nothing as easy as us tied
together, my clothes to yours—the gold
on my wrists the color of lion, tight as teeth.

Parvati Fails the First Test of Being Holy

A shivering under my skin
made me doubt, made me want
to lie down in the grass with you.

Late blooming and slim-shouldered,
I was always getting it wrong:
couldn't remember which hand

held the sickle, which the trident,
left my blessings to rust
in the rain. Ruined by nothing

but my thoughts, I wanted to be plain
and unconditional, so I could slip
unnoticed between this world

and the next—so I could dream
a body of my own with clever bones,
a new flutter for the heart.

Instead, I wilt every prayer
you put in me, crumple them,
petal-soft, under my rough tongue.

Parvati Tires of Waiting

Even the peacocks refuse to stay—only
gray-streaked birds, dumb and restless,
nip at my shoulders. See how well I suffer—
in puja for a hundred years, season after season
of my body's sweat-damped rind, of my lips'
chapped mantra of mud.

I have shunned music and salt, bathed
with the debris of dried leaves, unbound
my bun. It stands, strand after wiry strand,
errant and black as my will. I can line
your eyes with kajal, to protect against every
evil, offer you a dowry of plucked lotus,
their tongues a bitter blue. I can bribe
the holy out of you.

Parvati: A Wife's Mantra

It has taken me years to tempt you
from your holiness—your name
scrapes against thick-edged leaves,
against cave walls where I've
written my name in vermilion
so you won't forget.

I've called you out of your forest
into mine—see how the kitchen
glints the sharp silver of a mended
heart. It's sore and pinches every

so often. Hot hours in front of a stove,
the oil spits at me from a pan
like your mother's spite.
I mince garlic with hennaed
hands—a garden of orchids
blooming from wrist to thumb.

Under a sky pitted silver
we eat mangos that make
our throats itch, remind us
of the sweet pulp of first love.

The Goddess Left Behind

How easy to be left for damsel—when she
can lie unseen for days on a bed of thick
pine needles and not get pricked. Hold time
in place under her tongue, hold the last
flower of air in her chest to see what will happen—
what will bloom or wilt. When she can dream
and not be frightened of the years ahead of her
alone in myrtle and moss. When she can finally
see the animal's teeth for its shine and not
for the bite, the hurt it leaves on her.

The crows mournful at the mouth of the cave
she reads as a sign of leaving: the world empty
of her, she of clipped wings, glistening with
drama—so pretty to look at, so stiff with misuse.

Self-Portrait as a Girl Conceding

That boy who doesn't cut his hair—
who won't open his eyes when you

dance, you want him to like you
back, like you more. He can sit

in the rain as long as it takes, moving
his lips in a chant you're sure must

be holy. He's either praying or pretending
and you're fine with that. When he

opens his eyes and asks you to pierce
your nose, wash off that black eyeliner

before meeting his parents, you will
do anything, speak in the passive voice.

Never mind how pining doesn't suit—
bowing when you want to spit. He'll

tell you, *Get thinner*, so he can trace a map
of where your bones bend and become

sacred, where it hurts to be you. Skip
every lunch for an eternity, make a tether

from your hair so he can tie you
to his world. Hide the broken halo

of dead bees falling from your mouth
still tasting of small poisons.

Parvati Rewrites Myth

I won't miss the dirty hive of your hair,
your slow droning chant that lasts all day.
In this version, I'm done with kindness,

left it in my last life, with my cheap glass bangles
and cotton sari. I am my own constellation
of pathetic disasters, built my loneliness twig

by twig—lit it on fire to keep me warm. I can't
pretend to care, even as the butter burns to clear,
even as I never learned the names of trees.

Spiteful in white, I've lost the gold ringing
at my ankles. Enough with all this jungle, with
its shiny tongues, sloppy breath. I'll leave you

to your cave, your brilliance, spit your name
like paan from my cheek—walk out of
the tight cluster of trees, the sun's hot tone
beating my head like a drum.

Parvati Laments Her Reincarnation

My body a revision of bones, face
a dim-lit moon looking for its place
in the sky. How many times must we

rewind, start the story over? The stink
and heat of a wife's work stuck to my skin,
then you—smelling distant, of moss

and meadow. Each time we meet
something gets subtracted: the peculiar
beat of my blood, the browned husks

of my eyes. Read my palm, tell me where
to stand. Lie and say you hear the river
rushing through me, vein by vein.

Goddess Out of Favor

You ate leaves until your jaw ached
with ash, your spinster shoulders set

against the wind. You buried the names
you were once called beneath the brush.

It was never enough to fill the hole
your doubt dug. All those false steps

around the fire meant nothing. No one
held you up to the light, no sadness

glistened on your lips the pretty color
of persimmons, no one cared when

you walked into the forest raw and rustling
like sugar cane, your pulse thick with bees.

Destruction Myth

This time, death finds me at the rough hem
of the forest, a numb wish of a girl in need
of a tether, a goddess with her new sores
stitched closed. All the dark spaces between
my bones, traitors who dream of fire.

This time, I come back sullen with knots
in my veins, thorns on my tongue. I mistake
each ache and pinch for a love bite, all
those mistold stories for destiny.

You smell the heartache on my skin
like an old burn, want to break me
in half to find that jungle flushed
with green you lost me in, so you can
burn all the red out, turn me to white.

Unhappy Ending

You aren't like you used to be—hate the boy
who builds the world without you, who calls
you a goddess, woos you out of the jungle
then treats you like the second flower he sees.

You love the boy who pushes you back
toward the fire, who knows the only place
left for you is against bark and fern, against
shadows of all that burning. You become

a wilt that can't stop weeping sap, you vow
until you become an unkindness, until you sit
with his name crumbling hungry in your mouth.

Under the night's cold blink, you make your
dreams bigger than his sky, brighter
than his favorite constellation.

Part III

Goddess Erasure

Because the wood   my love
          is full of woes

Don't stray too far through
            the tangled wilderness

The nights are black and there are dangers
worse than you know

Creation Myth

Who said *god* and thought of me: the one
with a hundred skulls clattering at her throat—

necklace of little deaths, necklace of bony fate.
We are the reluctant who turn their backs

on wooded fires, on jeweled deer in headlights,
on turn-the-page romance that never gets past

first base. This is the world they feed you—
retouched, winsome and wooed. Only the good

get to heaven. Only the fairest get the goods:
The guy. The god. The eternal and everlasting.

Let shame seal my girl-lips against the wildness
until there is no one left to teach how *holy, holy*

breaks apart like honey in the mouth—the hum of incarnation
swarming my tongue, rising—unbearable—like a welt.

The Goddess as Jilted Lover

Think of the way you left me: with your fake
summer of half-thawed hives, uncertain blooms

budding and foolish. I have my own worries—
pressed into pleats, braided and obedient as

a schoolgirl. The trees full of gossips. I've been
second-guessed, second best, face chipped

by envy, put on the shelf to gather regret
in my prettied mouth. Thus, in my third

incarnation, I win Most Overlooked Goddess
though it's beyond me to charm. The new one

will get her way, so specific with spite, bullying
the breath out of me: loose-limbed, all the milk

in me gone. I've rinsed my dreams of you in a river
a hundred years wide, and still they are dry to the touch.

Because You Forgot Me, I Am Weird in the World

After all my wildness turned to white, only
a little bit of me wanted to be saved. Already
changed—wallflower, paper flower, I was
hidden and pressed, my soul a thin-slotted
door, an opening in the brush.

The forest crowds around me to stare—
blank-eyed, free of conscience. Those
eyes see what I've become: a bride
burning like her own planet.

The Goddess Shows up Late for the End-Of-The-World Party

Sari in a tear, face an ungodly mess, run of red
from one lip to the other. Over there

a blue-skinned flirt, a Krishna, looking
past me at the goddess from the next

lifetime, the one with the light eyes who
shows off her belly ring, swings her

baroque hips just so. Forsaken, reincarnated
beyond recognition, till I can't compete,

can't find each other on purpose:
on the dance floor or in print, the ink

on this love long dried. If you let me stay,
I'll let you cut your teeth on my heart

until it becomes a black forest beating
out of time, beating me out of this world.

Reconciliation

I.

He doesn't want her when
she's just a goddess practicing—
all fake and pious and pink.

Likes her better as a single girl
swearing in the old language
of dust and mud and stars.

Again, utter prayers that make
his skin glow the cool blue
neon, of the sagging sign
proclaiming *Karma* above the sad-sap
door of the bar—like all the doors
slammed shut at the end of the world.

He can feel the glare of the evil eye,
black on the back of his neck every
time she speaks, forgets how to protect
against it: was it salt or chilies
or mustard seeds—

but can anything prevent
that bitter bud of guilt
from blooming?

Another thing he lost in this incarnation.

II.

He didn't believe her
that nothing happened
with that other guy, the one
whose name means crying,
the one with ten heads and not
a pretty one in the bunch.

That monster who tried to touch
the black gasp of her hair, sniffing
the air behind her ear, looking
for that bit of her caught on
the wind: saffron and cinnamon—
her smell its own particular sin.

III.

He knows his doubt covers them
like unforgiving ash, how awful
the dirty itch of it between their fingers.

Nothing sacred about a fire
catching quick and ugly.

All this because she thought him
essential. Because she followed
him into that jungle. Fourteen years:

bored and bruised, how the animals
loved her less and less.

She'd tried—left clean sheets for him,
someone who rubbed coconut
oil into her scalp every morning.

Did he love her then? He can't recall.
Only, when he pulled at the tight knots
of her wrists, lead them into an ancient
meadow made wild with onion, all their
sour history turned to rot.

Their hands, plucked blooms, arms
pricked by thorns. He felt the sharp ache
of the cosmos expanding with its chant
and pulse, its stagger and stagger.

The Goddess Calls a Truce

For one night, I'll let myself be mistaken
for someone you once loved, give over

my heart like a night with no end. I won't
speak of my need to shimmer, of how

you didn't make room for me on the weary
grass that grows near your heart. My fingers,

inky from drawing birds all day, leave a trail
across your back, a blurred blessing in blue.

You insist we rip them in half, take to our bed.
All my good work undone. Even the season

is a sore disappointment: blooming when it
should freeze, snow melting to dull water.

I grow our loneliness in my mouth, feed you
sweet and bleak under a halo of buzzing stars.

The Goddess Tires of Being Holy

Call yourself whatever you want: *girl*
or *goddess*. Truth is, no one loves you
any better. There's not enough gold
in the world to make you feel holy, hallowed,
whole. No gloss pretty enough to save
a face marked by tragedy. For your trouble—
a handful of thorns, a bit of marigold dust.

This is what you get for begging to be
chosen: every god in the universe eyeing
you through the clouds like a hot wound
he can't help but press. That terrible beating
in your veins, so loud it makes your blood
hurt, that's the part you always get wrong—
the one where they watch you burn and burn.

The Goddess Reveals What It Takes to Be Holy

Every girl wants to be post-sadness,
post-jungle, so don't be fooled
by the cloak the color of heaven,
by petals perpetually at your feet.

To be the favorite, you have to
give in: clip on a smile, sweep
the floor with your braid, let him
call you by the wrong name.

Repeat after me: *I'll hurt for you,*
I'll domestic for you.
This requires constancy:
to shun, to burn, to look ugly

in white. Keep quiet, even as
the world ends—breath skipping
beats, histories peeled
from your palms, line by line:

first love, then life. Full of doubt,
you must be content with stitching
your own wounds, buffing your scars
to a blinding gleam.

Destruction Myth

When the world has me by its teeth,
it's what I deserve—the bite and bruise
of slack-jawed faith, tongue stuttering on
the names of gods, one nonsense syllable
at a time. Then, my prayers—blood-laced
wasp-heavy—dragged through dirt and honey

and pine are what I bring to be blessed.
I can sing like all the other girls, my lips
the wrong shade of martyr, my gold just
as bright. Each hunger starved. I want
to learn how to turn all these hurts holy
but no one speaks animal and leaf.

I mean to say *yes* but, in whispers,
everything ends up sounding like *death*.

Remnants of the Goddess

Let them come for what's left:
a chorus of bone, river, and soot.
Worthy enough. Holy enough.

Like all the others, singular—or not.
Wanting only for your name to blue
my lips and call it miracle.

Our love double-knotted, saddle stitched,
held the world together, until it didn't—
all the words you placed in me flushed
and faltered. From memory, I recited
their worn prattle—cut them clean
with my bite. The jungle we made in blame

grew and grew, fed on our melancholy.
Not even the birds knew to change their songs.

The Goddess Remade

You found me with night in my teeth—
a cheap date in need of a prayer, a myth,
a glass bangle in green. Any small mercy.

And I took it, leaving behind those
moaning cows, the thatched roofs
one lightning storm away from igniting.

You took inventory—breath and pulse,
cells and teeth, a numb womb.

You couldn't shake the river out of me,
so there it stayed, muddying my blood,
blurring the blink of my eyes.

Build me better—with a spine
stiff as bark, a mouth refusing to part,
caged by the brittle twigs of my ribs.

Build me, until there is nothing
soft left, nothing pink.

Dharma

Dig a cave, put your best goddess
in it. Call her by a new name.
Dress her as a red bride, then
a white widow.

Stitch her to the sticks on the ground
you call a bed with her hair's long, black
tinsel. Lay dull flowers at her feet,
the kind that limp and brown
with a look. Call this worship.

Pine for her. Tell her she is too beautiful
for this world. Accuse her pink mouth
of deception. Hold your hand tight
against her throat until it throbs
like a sun. Start again.

Notes

The following texts have provided a wealth of insight, both narrative and imaginative, to this book:

The Rāmāyana, Valmiki (abridged and translated by Arshia Sattar)
The Rāmāyana, Valmiki (translated by Ralph T. H. Griffith)
The Hindus: An Alternative History, Wendy Doniger
*Hindu Goddesses: Visions of the Divine Feminine in the Hindu
    Religions*, David R. Kinsley
Hindu Gods and Goddesses, W.J. Wilkins
The Goddesses' Mirror: Visions of the Divine from East and West,
    David R. Kinsley

"Goddess Erasure" (section I) is from the opening of the chapter, "Wilderness," from *The Rāmāyana*, translated by Arshia Sattar.

"Goddess Erasure" (section II) is from David Kinsley's *The Goddesses' Mirror: Visions of the Divine from East and West*.

"Goddess Erasure" (section III) is from Canto XXVIII, "The Dangers of the Wood," from *The Rāmāyana*, translated by Ralph T. H. Griffith.

"Self-Portrait as Goddess after the Fire" is based on the goddess Sati for whom the practice of a widow throwing herself on her husband's funeral pyre is named.

Acknowledgments

Grateful acknowledgment is made to the editors of the following publications in which these poems originally appeared, sometimes in earlier forms:

32 Poems: "A world like this hates" and "Novice"

Academy of American Poets' *Poem-a-Day*: "Remnants of the Goddess"

The Account: A Journal of Poetry, Prose, and Thought: "Reconciliation"

Birmingham Poetry Review: "Goddess Banished"

Colorado Review: "Unhappy Ending"

Connotation Press: An Online Artifact: "Parvati Practices Her Austerities," "Parvati Laments Her Reincarnation," and "Parvati Tires of Waiting"

Crab Orchard Review: "Parvati Rewrites Myth," "Sita in Exile" and "Goddess Remade"

Diode: "Parvati: A Wife's Mantra," "The Mother-Goddess Speaks of Her Regrets" (as "Krishna's Mother Speaks of Her Regrets"), "The Mother-Goddess Advises" (as "Krishna's Mother Advises"), and "Self-Portrait as Goddess after the Fire" (as "Sati")

Four Way Review: "Creation Myth [This is how the whole holy mess...]"

Guernica: "Sita Considers Her Rebellions"

The Journal: "In Captivity, Sita Contemplates Fidelity"

Hobart: "Self-Portrait as a Girl Conceding" (as "Goddess Diary #1"), "For Some Girls It's Impossible," "The Goddess Calls a Truce" and "Destruction Myth [When the world has me by its teeth...]"

Linebreak: "The Goddess Left Behind"

Memorious: "Why Sita Is Chosen" and "Parvati Fails the First Test of Being Holy"

The Missouri Review: "The Goddess Reveals What It Takes to Be Holy"

New England Review: "Monologue for a Goddess in Her First Incarnation" and "Goddess in the Dark"

Pleiades: "Fable" and "Destruction Myth [This time death finds me...]" (as "Death Finds Me")

Plume: "The Goddess Tires of Being Holy"

Prairie Schooner: "Hindu Mythology in Shorthand," "Sita's First Kiss with Suburban Landscape," "Destruction Myth [A ransom of tangled sari...]," "Because You Forgot Me, I Am Weird in the World," and "On the Eve of Being Reincarnated"

Passages North: "Prayer to Recognize the Body"

Poet Lore: "Dharma"

Pratik: "Creation Myth [You're a different kind of girl...]"

San Francisco Chronicle: "Creation Myth [Who said *god* and thought of me...]"

The Penguin Book of Indian Poets: "Prayer to Recognize the Body,"

"The Mother- Goddess Advises," "The Goddess Tires of Being Holy," and "The Goddess Reveals What It Takes to Be Holy"

Tupelo Quarterly: "The Goddess as Jilted Lover" and "The Goddess Shows up Late for the End- Of-The-World Party"

Some of these poems have appeared in a limited-edition chapbook, *The Goddess Monologues*, published by Diode Editions.

A big thanks to the wonderful people at Alice James Books, especially Carey Salerno, who made this book a reality.

Much gratitude to friends and mentors who've helped these poems through many different stages. I'm grateful to Blas Falconer and Karen Harryman for their years of support through makeshift residencies and long lunches and quick weekends away. Thanks to Kazim Ali for always making me think in new ways about poetry. A special thank you to Rita Dove who spent time with this book early on and lent it some magic. Thanks to Victoria Chang for her insights and friendship. Thank you to Paisley Rekdal for her constant support, friendship, and laughs. A special thank you to friends who continue to inspire: Angela Pneuman, Tarfia Faizullah, Allison Joseph, Jon Tribble, Helena Mesa, Traci Brimhall, and many, many more who have shaped my writing from the first lines.

Thank you to my family for their constant love and support, and especially to Jason, who is willing to take this journey with me, year after year, book after book.

Recent Titles from Alice James Books

Standing in the Forest of Being Alive, Katie Farris

Feast, Ina Cariño

Decade of the Brain: Poems, Janine Joseph

American Treasure, Jill McDonough

We Borrowed Gentleness, J. Estanislao Lopez

Brother Sleep, Aldo Amparán

Sugar Work, Katie Marya

Museum of Objects Burned by the Souls in Purgatory, Jeffrey Thomson

Constellation Route, Matthew Olzmann

How to Not Be Afraid of Everything, Jane Wong

Brocken Spectre, Jacques J. Rancourt

No Ruined Stone, Shara McCallum

The Vault, Andrés Cerpa

White Campion, Donald Revell

Last Days, Tamiko Beyer

If This Is the Age We End Discovery, Rosebud Ben-Oni

Pretty Tripwire, Alessandra Lynch

Inheritance, Taylor Johnson

The Voice of Sheila Chandra, Kazim Ali

Arrow, Sumita Chakraborty

Country, Living, Ira Sadoff

Hot with the Bad Things, Lucia LoTempio

Witch, Philip Matthews

Neck of the Woods, Amy Woolard

Little Envelope of Earth Conditions, Cori A. Winrock

Aviva-No, Shimon Adaf, Translated by Yael Segalovitz

Half/Life: New & Selected Poems, Jeffrey Thomson

Odes to Lithium, Shira Erlichman

Here All Night, Jill McDonough

To the Wren: Collected & New Poems, Jane Mead

Angel Bones, Ilyse Kusnetz

Alice James Books is committed to publishing books that matter. The press was founded in 1973 in Boston, Massachusetts to give women access to publishing. As a cooperative, authors performed the day-to-day undertakings of the press. The press continues to expand and grow from its formative roots, guided by its founding values of access, excellence, inclusivity, and collaboration in publishing. Its mission is to publish books that matter and preserve a place of belonging for poets who inspire us. AJB seeks to broaden our collective interpretation of what constitutes the American poetic voice and is dedicated to helping its artists achieve purposeful engagement with broad audiences and communities nationwide. The press was named for Alice James, sister to William and Henry, whose extraordinary gift for writing went unrecognized during her lifetime.

Designed by Pamela A. Consolazio

Spark
design

Printed by McNaughton & Gunn